Teesdale Villages and Countryside

in old picture postcards

by Vera Chapman

European Library ZALTBOMMEL/THE NETHERLANDS

BACK IN TIME

GB ISBN 90 288 6425 3

© 1997 European Library – Zaltbommel/The Netherlands

Introduction

The pictures in this album focus upon Teesdale as it was between 1880 and 1930. Arranged as a journey up the dale, they take us in an orderly progression through villages, farms and countryside along the river Tees and its tributary dales, starting near Abbey Gorge and reaching the head of the dale above the High Force.

From the North Sea to Cauldron Snout, the river Tees has formed for centuries the historic boundary between the North Riding of Yorkshire on the south and County Durham on the north. This continuity was broken in 1974, when a large slice of the North Riding was taken into County Durham. The two sides of the dale became united under the care of Teesdale District Council within the new County.

The Tees and its upper tributaries gather water from the high Pennines, with around 70 inches of rain per annum on the Cross Fell range. Notorious for its catastrophic floods, especially after heavy rains and melting snows, the river rises rapidly. At its worst, it sweeps down in a wall of water known as the Tees Roll, taking people by surprise on fords, banks, islands, waterfalls and bridges. Numerous stories of narrow escapes and drownings have been handed down. The Tees water, however, was reputedly good for dyeing. It also offered salmon, trout and coarse fishing until pollution around the estuary took its toll. The Tees and its tributaries provided power for watermills producing flour and grist, woollen and worsted cloth, carpets, linen thread and sawn timber. They also powered lead ore crushing plants and lead smelting mills. But moorland drainage, peat erosion and changes in the river's regime, together with the competition of steam power, brought the era of water power to an end. The silent mill by the stream became the idyll of artist and photographer. From the 1890s, water impounded in reservoirs on the Balder and Lune, and from 1970 on the Weel at Cow Green, brought a measure of control to the waters of the Tees.

In historic times, Teesdale remained something of a backwater, by-passed by the Romans as they forded the Tees heading for Stainmore and Carlisle, but raided by the Scots. The medieval mainstay was subsistence farming, with sheep and cattle on the common pastures and moors, and corn growing near the dale bottom almost to the High Force. From Tudor times, however, lead mining encouraged settlement beyond the High Force in a dual economy of miner-farmer families. In the 18th and 19th centuries the dale sides and upland commons were enclosed into fields for commercial farming and forestry. The dale reached its peak of population in the mid-19th century, after which, with falling lead prices and closing mines, the men transferred to local whinstone, limestone or sandstone quarries or moved with their families to coal mines, ironstone mines, blast furnaces, cotton mills or towns, or emigrated.

The lead industry affected the dale from the high moors down as far as Mickleton and Eggleston, but traditional farming remained important, with its focus at Middleton-in-Teesdale market. Further downstream, farming was probably dominant, and stately residences in parklands graced the scene. The focus here was Barnard Castle market and town, created by two Barnard Baliols in the 12th century and industrialised from the 18th century along the riverside in Bridgegate.

A new lifeline emerged somewhat belatedly in the mid-19th century with the coming of railways to Barnard Castle and thence to Middleton-in-Teesdale. Not only could quarry products be carried away. Dales people could commute to work in Bishop Auckland, Darlington and Teesside, and so could new residents. In the reverse direction, access to the beauties of the dale and its fresh air was now possible for families around the industrial estuaries of the Tyne, Wear and Tees.
The attractions of rambling, fishing and grouse shooting, waterfalls and moorland, blossom-filled meadows and botanical rareties, alpine flora and the little blue gentian all became more widely known. Villages evolved to provide for visitors, day-trippers, commuters and retired people.

With the loss of the dale's railways and the growth of car transport in the present century, these trends have been accentuated. Along came the Pennine Way, the Teesdale Way, defined pathways, old railway walks, caravan parks, nature reserves, field studies, adventure holidays and outdoor pursuits. The designation of Teesdale as an Area of Outstanding Natural Beauty, although belated, is a recognition of the dale's capacity to adapt to change without losing too much of its traditional character.

My thanks are due to those who kindly allowed me to copy their postcards or family pictures: Bessie Bell, Miss Dent (Hunderthwaite), E.G. Hounam, Gertrude Richardson, June Smith, Pamela Thomas, Dr. O.H. Wicksteed, Darlington Borough Museum and Darlington and Teesdale Naturalists' Field Club.

1   At the Meeting of the Waters where the Greta joins the Tees, members of Darlington and Teesdale Naturalists' Field Club pose on a field visit in 1929. The rivers carved gorges and rock pavements criss-crossed by deeply eroded joints. These facilitated medieval quarrying for local tombstones and fonts. The wooded gorges attracted famous artists and writers. Sir Walter Scott in 1812 wrote part of his epic poem 'Rokeby' in a cave beside the Greta. This river formed the boundary between Mortham and Rokeby, whose medieval villages both disappeared after Scottish raids in the 14th century. Above the bank at the rear, a few gravestones remain where Rokeby village church once stood. When Rokeby Park mansion was built and landscaped in the 18th century, a new Georgian church designed by Sir Thomas Robinson was built beside the turnpike road to Bowes, the present A66.

2 Morta's settlement, recorded in Domesday Book, was destroyed with its church and hall in the 14th century. By that time owned jointly with Rokeby, it was not until the late 15th century, however, that this handsome fortified tower house was built by Sir Thomas Rokeby. The corner turrets came later. Around the walled courtyard the 18th century buildings by Sir Thomas Robinson may have replaced earlier ones. After the Morritt family bought the combined estate, Rokeby Park became the main house and Mortham served for long as a farmstead. The latter was bought and restored shortly before the Second World War by William Rhodes-Moor- house, who was killed in the Battle of Britain. The charming sketch by A. Walker was made available as a postcard for visitors by Mrs. Rhodes-Moorhouse.

MORTHAM TOWER
Nr GRETA BRIDGE

3   Hroca's settlement, also recorded in Domesday Book and now a lost village, was bought from the Rokebys about 1610 by William Robinson of Brignall. The present mansion was built about 1730 to designs of William Wakefield, modified by the owner Sir Thomas Robinson, amateur architect and dilettante. He also enclosed and planted the park, but sold in 1770 to John S. Morritt. The balanced design of receeding cubes was intended as stables, kitchen wing and offices serving the house at the centre, with its grand saloon. Later modifications included the creation of a fine dining room in the west wing. John Bacon Sawrey Morritt, life-long friend of Sir Walter Scott, also entertained the artists Thomas Girtin, John Sell Cotman, J.M.W. Turner, A.W. Hunt, and writers John Ruskin and Robert Southey.

Rokeby Hall.   1963.

4   Abbey Bridge from its Yorkshire end was for many years a popular postcard subject. Built by John Sawrey Morritt in 1773-1774, the bridge soars over the Abbey Gorge near Egglestone Abbey in a single lofty arch. By the 1890s it was 'a beautiful structure, one bold arch, embattled parapets, covered with ivy'. Tolls are remembered as 6d for a horse and cart and $1/2$d for pedestrians. Children were free if they bought some sweets! The tollgate keeper sold lemonade and refreshments, but had to go across the road to bed, as each house had just one room! Tolls ended in 1957, and only the circular house foundations remain. Frank Atkinson talked to a lady whose uncle and aunt were tollkeepers. They slept on the strong webbing of dess or desk beds, also called press beds, which folded away into low cupboards. The bridge is now strengthened to cope with heavyweight traffic.

Toll Gate Abbey

5   Judging by the warm attire of the lady onlookers, the Honey-Manby war-time wedding in April 1916 took place on a cold day. On a hillside above the Tees at Startforth, Holy Trinity Church with its lofty spire is a well-known landmark. A church was recorded in the Domesday Book at Stradford, the ford on the Roman street. A succeeding church was demolished and rebuilt in 1863 in a Decorated Gothic style to the designs of J. and W. Hay of Liverpool for about £2,000. The hammer-dressed stonework can be seen in the picture. During the ceremony the happy couple would have faced the east window, a memorial to the Reverend Henry Kendall, the incumbent for forty years, who died in 1867. The smooth medieval font and inscribed slab to Sir Thomas de Bland and his wife are of the dark grey Tees marble from the Abbey Gorge.

6   Galgate lies on the line of the Roman road from Bowes Moor to the fort at Binchester. It forded the Tees at the wide shallows upstream from the later Norman castle and ascended via a gulley since filled in to the right of the church. Holy Trinity Methodist Church, built in 1894 on the site of four houses, makes an attractive ending to Galgate, enhanced by two lines of trees planted in 1873. Here, from the former early 19th-century police station on the left of the picture, the street widened out to house the livestock market for cattle, sheep and pigs. This moved out to a Mart in Vere Road in 1890. Lower Galgate was still partly residential, with probably fewer shops than now, but it had a share of the thirty pubs and inns reported in the town in 1850. After all, this was the route of two turnpike roads: Stockton to Barnard Castle from 1747 and Sunderland Bridge to Bowes from 1748.

Galgate, Barnard Castle.

Maggie is spending the week end with me here. Hope you are having good times

7   One of the lines of trees has gone from Galgate, giving way for motorised transport. The picture would be taken about 1928, when buses served the town from several directions. The light-coloured bus was the most recent. The second from the left had narrow hard tyres. Behind is a shop with a barber's pole outside. The Commercial Hotel on the left was one of 26 hotels and inns still in town in the 1890s, despite the efforts of the Temperance Movement. Its influence can just be detected beside the trees in the form of a Gothic drinking water fountain, erected in 1874 and topped by a gas lamp. The tall building on the right was briefly the home of Roderick Impey Murchison, eminent geologist and explorer. Just beyond it are the premises later demolished for access to a public car park. Also on this side, one of the lower premises became the Scala cinema.

82501.   BARNARD CASTLE, GALGATE.

8   Horsemarket curved and widened into Market Place. Here were sited the Toll Booth and Shambles (butchers' stalls), until removed about 1808. An old Town Guide stated that until the 1830s Bluestone House also stood in the middle of Market Place. This picture of about 1930 shows that a slip road has narrowed the cobbles. The premises on the right with their long back yards were laid out in the early 12th century and faced the curving castle wall and moat. The left was open ground until the ruined castle was dismantled in the 17th century. The Golden Lion is dated 1679. The mock beams on the outside reflect the real low-beamed ceilings inside. The town houses of local families became shops. The bank on the left, now Nat West, formerly housed the Hanby family. The Raby Arms was the town house of the Lords Barnard. The Richardsons' house became in 1880 Young's jewellers, now Hopper's.

MARKET PLACE, BARNARD CASTLE. 221624

9   Taken from the south end of Market Place, this earlier picture shows the wide cobbled area before the sliproad was inserted. The Witham Hall, with flag flying, was built by subscription in memory of Henry Witham of Lartington Hall, who helped found a Mechanics' Institute and supported a Dispensary for the poor. Just beyond it are the premises demolished for the new bank building on the right of picture number 8. A feature of this street scene are the signboards, often at roof level. On the far right is Walter Willson, well-known chain grocer. The Angel Hotel on the left by the carts was demolished for a one-storey Woolworths. Behind the horse-drawn coach is the extension to the old King's Head coaching inn. Through the archway was the entrance to the castle.

10 The fine sweep of Georgian frontages reflects that period's prosperity. Extra doorways led into long rear yards, former farmyards, which became overcrowded with workers' housing when the riverside industries were flourishing. Well Yard in Horsemarket, for example, had 19 houses. On the left is the Turk's Head inn from which, in 1804, a gamekeeper and a militia man targeted the weather vane on the Butter Cross to prove who was the better shot. Next door is Walter Willson (wholesale and retail), latterly Barmby's. Barnard Castle is noted for retaining its period shop fronts, although few have kept their ornate iron rails above the shop windows as seen here. At the end of the row is Backhouse & Co's Bank, now Barclays, built in 1878 to the design of Darlington architect G.G. Hoskins. It replaced one large and some smaller houses or shops.

11 By this time the slip road and public toilets have been made and the Newgate entry at the Butter Cross widened. The proud three-storey King's Head Hotel is an obviously more recent building than its neighbours. A pen and ink sketch of its predecessor shows a coach arch on the left, next to the surviving original inn which has a small porch. Here, in 1838, stayed Charles Dickens when he came to investigate the notorious boys' boarding schools of the district. Known as the Yorkshire or London schools, they are said to have soon closed down after Dickens published his 'Nicholas Nickleby' book based on them. Dotheboys Hall at Bowes is the best known.

KING'S HEAD HOTEL AND MARKET CROSS, BARNARD CASTLE.   221623

12 The Market Cross or Butter Cross dated 1747 was by Thomas Breaks, a local man who worked in woollens and bought nearby Sledwich in 1720. How much of the Cross he built is uncertain. The stonework of the two storeys has weathered differently. The canopy is by consensus a later addition, at times railed, boarded or walled in. Its many uses include a place where farmers' wives sold their butter, eggs, cheese and poultry on Wednesdays, a town hall, a court room with a gallery for the jury and a lock-up below, a fire engine depot, a shop, a shelter and a meeting and exhibition room. The cupola houses the old market or fire bell. The weather vane has two shot holes in it! The corner shops in Dickens' time were those of a solicitor and of Humphrey the clockmaker featured in 'Master Humphrey's Clock'. Their demolition in the 1930s opened up Newgate and St. Mary's parish churchyard entrance. The bank's cast iron railings have now gone.

THE CROSS. BARNARD CASTLE

13 This postcard sent in 1913 is one of many of Blagraves House. They record changes in stonework, windows, paving and use. Listed grade I, the oldest surviving house in Barnard Castle, its recognised date is the 16th century with a possible medieval core. Its vaulted cellars have a deep well and a passage leading under the road. The tower bay was added in the 17th century, but its crumbling stonework was patched in 1979-1980. The Tudor doorway was supplemented in the 18th century by the upper door. It was probably here that Cromwell consumed 'burnt wine and oatcakes' on his town visit in 1648. In the 17th century the Blagraves altered the interior, leaving a plaster ceiling with a date 1672 and oak beams carved into flowers and fruit. The house has variously been a home, an inn, tenements, a ropemaker's and a museum. Since the Second World War it became a restaurant.

Balgrove's House, Barnard Castle

14 Local people and visitors remember Blagraves House as a museum in the 1920s and 1930s. Then named Cromwell House, that was when the stone musicians were placed on the ledge across the front. A coat of armour was strung high up on the side of the tower, and various antique objects displayed on the small forecourt during opening hours. There was also a set of wooden stocks for two, complete with its bench. At that time the window immediately below the musicians was still a three-light mullioned window like the smaller ones on the upper storey. Inside was a room with a fine stone Tudor fireplace in a panelled semicircle fitted with curved benches, a bedroom with a carved four-poster bed, and a chamber of horrors! Postcards were issued.

15 This snowy scene looking over County Bridge to the fields of Startforth beyond was taken from the path which leads to the riverside where the Percy Beck joins the Tees. The gas works, the buildings along Bridgegate and Bridge End Mill on the right have all gone since the Second World War. New housing now covers most of the distance. The gas works, built in 1835, had two gasholders framed in by latticed bars and a retort house with a tall chimney. During excavation for the foundations, a paved roadway was found on line with Galgate and the Roman road from Binchester to Bowes which forded the Tees in the foreground of the picture, where the river is wide and shallow.

The Sills, Barnard Castle.

16   Barnard Castle began soon after 1095 when Guy Baliol of Picardy built a timber castle and rock-cut ditch on the site pictured here. In the 12th century, two Barnard Baliols built the stone castle with a moat and a curtain wall enclosing seven acres. The new town, market place, church and town fields were also created then. These ruined buildings in the Inner Bailey were a 14th century rebuilding of the Great Hall, private apartments and round tower during the tenure of the Earls of Warwick. The mullioned oriel window is attributed to the Duke of Gloucester who became Richard III. After the ruined castle was bought by Sir Henry Vane about 1626, stone was taken to renew Raby Castle. Later an orchard and gardens occupied part of the grounds, a bearded man dressed as a hermit or monk guided visitors, lead shot was manufactured in the tower and the Hall housed a tannery.

Barnard Castle.

17   This panoramic view upstream from High Startforth shows Bridgegate crowded with industrial premises and houses, most of which were demolished in the 1950s. In the 18th century, Barnard Castle's industries were woollens and worsteds, tammies and stockings, dyeing and tanning, leather and bridles based on local sheep and cattle. Weaving was done in lofts with weavers' lights, and weirs fed water-powered mills. By the early 19th century, woollens having declined, flat-weave carpet making developed in seven mills employing up to 400, but by mid-century it, too, was declining and soon ended. Dunn's mill and dyehouse fronted the river near the bridge. Raine's mill, which survives as Bridgegate Tyres, is near the end of the weir. Monkhouse's is now Booksale. Meanwhile, linen shoe thread spinning developed at Bridge End Mill on the left and became the main employer.

Barnard Castle

18   Houses at the Durham bridge-end have given way to grassy slopes and the crumbling castle wall has been consolidated. The ruined wall at river level was the dye-house below Dunn's carpet factory. Tees water was renowned for excellent dyeing. The upper storey of the White Swan Inn on the left still retains its weavers' lights, partly blocked. Low water reveals the rocks which caused the bridge to be built here and the old ford abandoned. County Bridge with its five broad ribs is credited to the 13th or 14th century. It was damaged during the Rising of the North against Queen Elizabeth in 1569 and again in the great flood of 1771, when cottages and land were swept away and the parapets had to be replaced. A chantry chapel at the centre also vanished. Never widened, the bridge has survived ever increasing and weightier traffic, now controlled by lights and weight restrictions.

Castle and Bridge Barnard Castle

FRITH
BC.149

19   Harrison Ullathorne & Co's Bridge End spinning mill at Startforth began in 1798 as a flax and tow mill making linen stitching thread for boot and shoe manufacturers in Britain and France. It also made saddlers' twine, rope, binder twine and string. Drying racks and ropewalk can be seen in picture 21. This illustrated label is a romantic version of the mill and its environs, depicted after the railway reached the upper part of Barnard Castle town in 1858. The trains could scarcely have passed below the castle which perches above a direct drop to the river! The mill buildings appear to have developed in stages. A weir directed water into the mill. It used water power, as mentioned in a directory of 1829, as well as steam. A tailwater arch and a chimney base survive. The firm also had a smaller flax mill farther downstream on the other bank of the Tees.

20 Ullathorne's mill employed around 400 men, women and boys and was the main employer after the demise of the carpet trade. Former employees recalled a 60-hour working week. After the First World War it gradually declined, ending with 100 workers doing one week on and one week off. It closed in 1932. The buildings housed soldiers returning from Dunkirk, and then remained empty. After the war the mill was bought by a local farmer and used as a mushroom farm, manure store, poultry-packing station and lemonade plant until 1962. Blanco blocks for canvas shoes were a side line. His widow lived in a flat inside the mill. No viable use was found for the deteriorating complex. Despite Listing in 1974, this prominent landmark complementing the castle across the river was demolished in 1975. The chimney base, mill-race wall and items of machinery are retained as reminders on the site, now grassed over.

21 This version of an often photographed view from the castle crag captures the long ropewalk shed and hanks of linen shoe thread drying on racks at Ullathorne's mill. The weir directed water into the mill race behind the wall. On the left is Lartington Hall Park which ends at the Startforth boundary along Deepdale Beck, which enters the Tees near the aqueduct. The distant high-level viaduct at 132 feet above the Tees had a lattice-work girder superstructure mounted on four stone piers. It carried the South Durham and Lancashire Union Railway opened in 1861 from a new station at Barnard Castle over Stainmore summit at 1,436 feet to Kirkby Stephen and Tebay. A link in the iron trade for coal and coke to west Cumberland and high grade iron ore and limestone to Teesside, it closed in 1962. From 1868, the Tees Valley line had branched off at Lartington, but closed in 1964. Of the Tees viaduct demolished in 1972, only the stone abutments remain.

RIVER TEES, BARNARD CASTLE

22 The aqueduct at Flatts Woods was built by the Stockton and Middlesbrough Water Board in 1893 to carry water from Hury and Blackton reservoirs, then under construction in Baldersdale. Massive iron pillars support the latticework rails and water pipes, which were boarded over as a footbridge. Battlemented turrets at the ends were doubtless to blend with the castle! The girl and dog stand on a limestone outcrop with rectangular joint patterns. This area, where the Percy Beck joins the Tees, was developed for recreation with seats and a paddling pool. Rustic walks along Percy Beck still lead up into Galgate via Raby Avenue and Flatts Road. The girl faces upstream along Flatts Woods, where Dr. George Edwards, with permission from the Earl of Darlington, created pleasant walks to a riverside spa or chalybeate spring located by its sulphurous smell. It no longer runs.

23 Cotherstone's East Green is crossed by West Beck in a stone-lined channel. Manor House on the left, formerly Mount Pleasant Farm, is believed to be the oldest house in the village. It dates from 1600, and was improved about 1700 and 1750. The far end is a recent extension. The gable end of the heather-thatched house next door became a butcher's shop, one of fifteen shops in the village. Just before the church, the Temperance Hall of 1893, enlarged in 1927, is now the Village Hall. St. Cuthbert's Church was built in 1881 by Messrs. Kyle, builders of the Bowes Museum. A peal of six bells was a gift. The short spire was replaced by the tall, slender spire, now a local landmark. The church school of 1894 opened by Claude, 13th Earl of Strathmore and Kinghorne, became the Church Hall and is now a house. The road leads to Cotherstone Moor, an open Common Regulated by an Act of 1867. Set back beside the house on the right was a smithy.

24   Nicholson Terrace on the left of Cotherstone's main street was built in the 19th century, but incorporates datestones of 1775 and IN1682 on the gable end. It replaced a large Georgian house with a pedimented doorway, used as a boarding school ('one of the worst sort') and later as a house owned by Anthony Nicholson. The Red Lion has TH1758 on its lintel. It remained heather-thatched until 1935, and was much photographed. Mr. Birkitt remembers it being rethatched in the 1920s by Tommy Donald, then aged about 60. Its steep pitch was retained when finally flagged.

The distant house Belle Vue later became a post office, newsagent and general store, with a doorway cut across the corner and a shop window facing the street. Since her fame after TV's 'Too Long A Winter', Hannah Hauxwell retired to it from her farm at the head of Baldersdale.

25 The Congregational Chapel on the right, built in 1869 to seat 160, was closed about 1940 and served as a garage and warehouse until converted to a house, Chapel Villa. It superseded an older building of 1748, thought to be the first Congregational chapel in Teesdale. A bungalow now adjoins the former chapel. This card was posted in 1911. The heather-thatched house and byre burned down in 1912. Only the doorway with a lintel MH1725 is left of the house, but the byre was rebuilt in 1963 as a garage and shop. Wetherby House was Tyreman s joiner's business, whilst Porch Cottage, at the pavement edge, was the living part for a fruit and vegetable shop, now Lynton, thought once a chimney sweep's. The distant Wesleyan Methodist Church with a date plaque 1872 was built of Shipley quarry stone forded by horses and cart across the Tees via Hagg Lane.

Cotherstone

26 This view of the 1725 thatched house, burned down in 1912, was taken from the Red Lion. The tiny windows had sideways sliding Yorkshire sashes. An elderly man re-calling his mid-19th century Cotherstone boyhood remarked that 'there could not be a more dreary spot on earth' as so many properties were still heather-thatched. This 'black thack' had to be replaced after about twenty years. Common heather (cal-luna vulgaris) was gathered from the moor and laid in bundles called threaves row by row from the eaves upwards. The bundles were pegged down with bent hazel twigs known as spelks or lig-gers. Older properties had common rights to get stone, heather, peat and turf. Perhaps Cotherstone kept to its thatch so late because the common remained unenclosed and came in close to the village. Flagstone replacements were called 'thackstones'. The pan-tiles at Wetherby House are unusual so far up the dale.

27 Cotherstone became a holiday resort when the Tees Valley Branch Railway reached the dale in 1868. A close connection grew up with Sunderland, which led to the nickname Little Sunderland. Boarding and apartment houses and cafés emerged to cater for visitors. There were also several large houses and villas old and new, and commuting to Darlington, Teesside and Bishop Auckland developed. These changes probably increased the need for domestic servants, an important outlet for the girls of families. This postcard was probably sent early this century 'Wishing you the Compliments of the Season' probably by the young lady in the photograph. She was Laura 'in service at Cotherstone' and came from Newbiggin.

28 This is a Hounam family group at Cotherstone. They lived for a time at Cherry Tree Cottage which bordered the main street with a front garden near the present-day post office. Grandpa George Hounam served 54 years at Backhouse's bank in Sunderland and was its manager in the 1890s. The brothers William, E.S. and G.L. Hounam were taking local photographs in the village around 1890 in the period when Hury reservoir was being built. The group includes Grandma Hounam and an aunt of E.G. Hounam.

29 Voting day at Cother-
stone. The horse and trap is
standing outside a 'Commit-
tee Room', which can be
recognised as the house next
to Gill the butcher's shop,
which has recently closed. It
is opposite Cherry Tree Cottage, where the Hounams
lived for a while.

30 Fox Hall is depicted here as 'G. HODGSON' THE PEOPLE'S GROCERY AND PROVISION STORE', and an 1890 Directory lists George Hodgson, grocer. The shop is now remembered as Willie Hodgson's grocery, selling everything from fire shovels to syrup on tap from a barrel. At the rear was a carpenter's workshop from which tools were donated to the Bowes Museum. Fox Hall ceased to be a shop in 1964. Rosemary Thompson has recently restored the front to its original design. The main part of the house is thought to date from the early 1600s. There are flagged floors and adzed roof timbers. The rear teefall is dated RBM 1747, and may have replaced an outside stone staircase or stair turret.

31 Looking towards Cotherstone's West Green the Wesleyan Methodist Chapel was built in 1872 using fine stone from Shipley quarry and stone from Jacob Allison's former carpet factory beside Balder Bridge. The day school at the rear opened in 1874 and closed in 1964. The adjoining row of five houses included South View, a bread and cake shop and haberdashers, and Holmdale House was Robinson's boot and shoemaker's shop and apartment house. The single-storey cottage opposite, formerly a farm, was for many years a bakery and café, Ye Tea House. It is well remembered as The Kettle from its hanging sign with steam from the bakery oven emerging from the spout. The distant gable-fronted Greystones replaced an old farm. Saltoun House and West Lodge were formerly a chapel and school owned by the Trustees of the Methodist Meeting, which had begun as a stable barn chapel opened in 1777 by John Wesley.

Cotherstone.

32 This photograph is entitled 'The Young Folks at Cotherstone'! On the left are William Harle and his wife, Mary Ann Ramsay. On the right are her brother William Ramsay and his wife. Mr. F.G. Holmes, great-grandson of William Harle, thinks that either William Harle (born 1828 at Gateshead, became a colliery manager at Page Bank and died 1891 at Durham), or his son Richard (born 1850 at Wylam and buried in Cotherstone churchyard) built Hagg House, which is situated beside the lane leading from West Green to The Hagg and the Tees ford. The house itself began as a single-storey stone cottage, had a brick two-storey house added on and the cottage raised to two storeys more recently. A family story tells that William used bricks given to him by Bell Brothers. Another tells that Richard built it for his father and lived there later.

The Young Folks at Cotherstone

33 Tees Mill, Cotherstone, stands a little downstream from the Balder confluence, Hagg Lane and the Tees ford. A weir set obliquely across the Tees pointed water directly into the corn mill at the water's edge behind the house, as seen in this postcard sent with a George V halfpenny stamp. The mill probably ceased to grind in the late 1890s and was said to have been made into cottages about 1897 The flat land or Holme was at one stage a tennis court, and members of the Hounam family played tennis there. Tees watermills tended to finish working about the turn of the century, when moorland drainage affected the river flow and there was competition from steam. In 1890 William Kipling had a grocer's shop in the main street with a steam corn mill behind, which worked into the 1920s and 1930s.

TEES MILL, COTHERSTONE.

34   Balder Mill or Doe Park Mill stood on the west side of the river a little upstream from Balder Bridge. Here the river descends quickly over rock outcrops, allowing a stone-lined leat to be led over the adjacent pasture to drop water on to the wheel at a high breast-shot or pitch-back position. This was a more efficient use of water power than overshot or undershot wheels. It is clearly demonstrated in this post-card, one of many showing the picturesque mill in va-rious stages of decay, a scene also romantically portrayed by artists. It seems to have gone out of use about the turn of the century, perhaps affected by the building of the Baldersdale reservoirs. By 1808 the miller's house behind was in ruins. The stor-age building on the left has now nearly gone. The roofless mill is a shell with one huge grit millstone on the floor.

Balder Mill, Cotherstone

35 'Viewing of the Pipe Track at Hury' is another of the Hounam family records of the district. The shadows show that the surveyors for the building of the Stockton and Middlesbrough Water Company's Hury reservoir are looking down dale towards Cotherstone on the south side of the deep channel of the Balder. The building of Hury began in 1884. Up to 90 feet deep and 1.5 miles long, with 36 inches of annual rainfall, it was commissioned ten years later, in 1894. Meanwhile Blackton reservoir, a mile long and up to 60 feet deep, with 41 inches was completed in 1896. The water from Hury and Blackton reservoirs was led off to Lartington filter beds and across the Tees by an aqueduct built in 1893 (see pictures 21 and 22). Baldersdale farms lost their better in-bye land.

36 'Team of Horses Dragging a Large Pipe for the Pipe Track' is another Hounam picture of the period 1884-1896. The immense construction work by man power and horses over a period of twelve years brought a migratory workforce who were accommodated in a shanty town of wooden huts in Baldersdale, located amongst the farms between Cotherstone village and the new Hury dam. The population of Cotherstone increased in the decade 1881-1891 from 638 to 940 and dropped back to 665 a decade later. On the north side of the dale, a similar rise and fall occurred at Hunderthwaite, from 285 to 440 and back to 282, perhaps accommodated on the farms.

37 This photograph of Hunderthwaite Farm was taken about 1930. The heather-thatch was replaced in 1938, retaining the steep pitch of the now slated roof. The house was built in 1730 by William Dent, and followed the traditional northern building style. There is no front door. A cross-passage separates the house and byre and gave entry to each. The house itself is of cruck frame construction. The farm buildings on each gable end are later buildings or rebuildings with exterior doorways and stone-flagged roofs of a gentler pitch. The house faces south and backs on to Hunderthwaite village street, formerly a green. Across the green were the ruins of another similar farmstead Hunderthwaite and Bowes Moor remained unenclosed until 1859.

38 Many dales villages had their own Show. These were social occasions, but few survived beyond the 1930s. The sheep here are being judged at Hury Show in Baldersdale. Other social occasions were the Shepherds' Meetings. Sheep, usually heufed through generations to a particular part of a moor, could stray long distances along unenclosed moorland. At Shepherds Meetings held regularly at locations on the fringes of the North Pennines, stray sheep could be reclaimed. They were identified by their owner's sheep marks in the form of horn burns, ear clips or wool marks as recorded in Flock Books.

Hury Show. Baldersdale.

39 This card of Romaldkirk, posted in 1906, is a view over the upper village by the railway station, down Fell Lane to the green and church, with Eggleston Common in the background. The single-track Tees Valley Branch Railway opened in 1868 and closed in 1964, when single fares to Barnard Castle were 1/-. Seven stopping trains per weekday in each direction are remembered. There were a goods yard and coal staithes. In earlier days, lead from Eggleston smelt mill used to be carted here. The station building near the signal is now a house. Nearby Bunker Hill Cottage recalls an American War of Independence battle near Boston in 1775 when the rebels were defeated. A house lintel is dated 1740, and the protruding Wesleyan Methodist Chapel of 1869 is now a house. The house next door has an inscription William 19 L 02 Kipling with 17 PT 90 below. The villa Carrowcroft next door protrudes above the other roofs.

Romaldkirk.

40 Carrowcroft, its more usual spelling, stands above the high end of Romaldkirk green. This view was taken from Fell Lane, and is now obscured by the trees and bushes which ring the grounds. The ornate iron railings on the garden wall went for scrap during the Second World War. The villa was built in 1875 as his own residence by William Kipling, a member of an old Teesdale family mentioned as early as the 15th century. In the 1920s and 1930s it was the home of Dr. Hawthorn.

CARROCROFT
ROMALDKIRK.

41 This view from Middle Green to High Green taken around the turn of the century has changed in little but detail. Beyond the main road crossing, the front garden of the house on the right was later covered over by a long glass veranda. Rose Cottage on the far left still has a low bulge on its gable end, indicating that a beehive bread oven had been built into the thickness of the wall beside the fireplace. Peat, sticks or coals from the fire would be burnt on the brick-oven floor. When heated through, the oven would be cleaned out (in Teesdale with a bundle of rags tied to a stick called a malin). Baking went on by the residual heat The pleasant stone doorway inscribed 17 IWP 32 is now obscured by a large stone vestibule.

ROMALDKIRK, NEAR BARNARD CASTLE.

№1095.

42 Posted in 1912, this view from Fell Lane captures the new stone Reading Room and Billiard Room built 'To the Memory of King Edward VII' (who died in 1910) and later enlarged. The Toby Tree adjoins it. In the centre distance the Kirk Inn had a cobbler's next door. High Green seems newly mown or scythed. On Middle and Low Greens Romaldkirk Fair was held in Spring and Autumn for cattle, sheep and horses. Begun in 1807 by the Rector, Reginald Bligh, it ended in 1930. There were stalls, a roundabout and a traction engine. A toffee stall is remembered. The greens were part of the common grazings. A pinfold for stray animals has now been renovated beside Beer Beck. Fines were 1d for a horse and $\frac{1}{2}$d for a beast or sheep. The pinder was paid from grazing rentals. By the 1930s, with traffic a problem, grazing lapsed. Pumps are preserved on High and Low Greens. Piped water did not arrive until 1934.

Romaldkirk

43 There were four inns in Romaldkirk, not surprising as St. Romald's Church, here obscured by trees, served one of the most extensive parishes in England. The Rose and Crown with a lintel IHM 1735 now has a glazed extension. The recess beyond is no longer railed or cobbled. The other building, now a house, was The King's Arms, with a mounting block by the door and its sign on the gable end. There was a hatch for lowering barrels to the cellars. Formerly it was The Blue Bell, where manorial courts were held in Georgian times. The Kirk Inn opposite the church gates still operates, but the Mason's Arms has gone. There was a brewery at Rose Style from 1824 until the end of the 19th century. On the right, men are sitting under the Toby Tree, a large sycamore named after Tobias Bayles (who died in 1652) and on which public notices were displayed. Its site is now marked by a conifer and rockery.

ROMALDKIRK, NEAR BARNARD CASTLE.

Nº 1096

44 William Hutchinson built the first Romaldkirk almshouses or hospital in 1674. In his will in 1693 he endowed it and a school at Bowes as a charity. The beneficiaries were six men or women from villages in the parish. They had to be over 60 years of age, poor, Protestant, attend church on Sundays, and be in their houses by 9.00 p.m. in summer and 7.00 p.m. in winter. The premises were rebuilt in 1829 and are now known as Hutchinson Terrace, recently converted to three dwellings and with less stringent requirements. The ornate pump with its gargoyle-like spout graces the front garden below an inscription on the central pediment. The piece of wall in the bottom corner of the picture is Beer Beck bridge. Saxon 'beer' and Norse 'beck' both mean 'a stream'.

ROMALDKIRK, NEAR BARNARD CASTLE.

№ 1094.

45 The Lune, joining the Tees below Mickleton, was crossed from 1869 by the sturdy viaduct of the Tees Valley Branch Railway. At Mickleton the Lune powered the Atkinsons' corn mill until the wheel broke in 1929, and a fulling mill for linen cloth. Laithkirk church served Lunedale, Mickleton, Lonton and Holwick as a chapel of ease to Romaldkirk from the 15th century until separated in 1845. A simple barn church, it was enhanced in 1898, and a vicarage built. The Queen Mother, as Lady Elizabeth Bowes-Lyon and later with the Duke of York, attended service here when visiting Teesdale. Lunedale had three inns, at Grains o'th Beck, Bowbank (Pol House Inn) and Laithkirk. The last was inscribed WJB 1779 and 'If you go by, And dry you be, The fault's in you, And not in me'.

GREETINGS FROM
MICKLETON
LAITHKIRK
LUNE BRIDGE AND VIADUCT
LAITHKIRK CHURCH INTERIOR
RIVER LUNE
MN.24.
THE MILL

46 These Mickleton houses face the Rose and Crown. On the left is Ronnie Raine's post office. Mickleton, a roadside village now about a mile long, was centred on its green until this was enclosed with the town fields, pastures and moor in 1808. It was a workaday village with farmsteads, small houses, cottages and numerous shops. Men worked at the local whinstone and limestone quarries, at lead mines in Lunedale and around Middleton, and as railwaymen and labourers. Thatch, once prevalent, had gone before 1914. There were three inns in the village. Two closed before the First World War, the General Wolfe at Quebec Terrace and the Black Bull at the west end, which became two cottages. Only the Rose and Crown survived, but a Blacksmith's Arms has newly opened. Despite the completion of Grassholme reservoir in 1914, piped water arrived in Mickleton only in the 1950s. A public pump, not in use, is preserved beside the main road.

47 High Green farmhouse, Mickleton, bears a lintel 'John and Mary Dent 1752'. The Dents have lived in Mickleton for about five hundred years. Their occupation of High Green ended after the deaths of Tom in 1986 and his wife Mollie. By the early 17th century the Dents were the major landholders and keepers of the manorial chest. It was here that Tom and Mollie Dent during the 1960s allowed the author to study the Mickleton Enclosure Award, its two maps each as large as the double bed! The house front conceals an early 17th century single-storey longhouse with a living room, cross passage and byre, all raised later to two storeys with a rear stair turret. In 1752 it was refronted and given a rear range and new staircase, the old byre becoming the parlour. This picture, taken by the author on a visit by the N.E. Vernacular Architecture Group, shows some of the period features retained to the present day.

48 The Lunedale or Hury Show is another of the dales' shows that has ceased. This card was posted in 1907. High Force, Middleton-in-Teesdale, Winston and Barnard Castle also lost theirs. Only Eggleston Show still runs.

THE SHOW, GRAIN'S O' BECK.

49   Eggleston Show in 1910 was a well-dressed occasion. The signs on the church tea tent read: 'Tea with bread and butter and cakes, 9d each. Tea with ham sandwiches, bread and butter and cakes 1/- each.' Agricultural, poultry and flower shows in the 1890s were held annually at the new Reading Room in the village. In recent years the show has been held on the Haughs, the level area by Eggleston bridge. Tom Dent of High Green, Mickleton, was for long a leading light. The show now continues at High Shipley. Harold Beadle, formerly of Dale House, relates that the Methodist circuit tent was let out to cater for refreshments at events such as agricultural shows to raise money for the circuit. The name Eggleston derives from a personal name Ecgwulf not from ecclesia, although a church existed prior to 1500, probably near the Hall. The present Holy Trinity Church was built in 1869 in a newly-formed parish.

Eggleston Show 1910

50   Eggleston Post Office was located until about 1910 at the house with the trellised porch. In the 1890s the postmaster was William Robert Walker. Letters arrived at 8.55 a.m. and were despatched at 4.20 p.m. The letter and parcels cupboards remain, but windows have been altered. On the right the board reads Grocer, Coates, Draper, but in the 1890s Henry Coates was a shoemaker, draper and milliner. Alice Davidson and her mother later ran the shop. In the 1960s it was a grocery and sweets shop with a paved forecourt and two large shop windows fitted for exterior sun blinds. About 1980 it was converted to a house. The cottages below are also now renovated. A public pavement has been made, the green is not railed, the grass is mown and there are seats. The man with two buckets would be carrying water from the public tap on the green. This and a water trough for animals are preserved.

No 1090   EGGLESTONE POST OFFICE
                           NEAR BARNARD CASTLE.

51 Ducks are settled on The Green, which is a private space belonging to the houses around it on the east side of the village. The man and boy on the left are on a motor bike and sidecar. The man in the group on the right is wearing plus-fours. The people in the picture are probably members of the Bainbridge family. The right-hand cottage still has older style sashes, whereas the other houses have later ones. The stone flag roofs are typical of Teesdale, with coping stones down the gable ends. The taller house has slightly ornate corner stones or kneelers, which prevent the heavy coping stones from sliding down, especially on exposed gables.

52   Gordon Terrace, now Gordon Bank, is beside the Moor Road which rises steeply from Eggleston village to Hill Top and the Moor Cock Inn. The name may be a topical one, after General Charles Gordon who, after serving as a soldier and diplomat in many parts of the world, was killed at Khartoum in 1885. These houses were built as back-to-backs. Most are now converted into through houses facing across Teesdale over this former field which is now divided into gardens. Eggleston Moor, to the north of the village, was enclosed by Acts of Parliament in 1785 and 1816, and the old route along the Moor edge defined. The road led to the London Lead Company's smelting mill at Blackton Beck which closed in 1905, and over to Stanhope in Weardale. A Peat Road leading up the moor from beside the Moorcock Inn was set out for villagers with common rights to continue to dig for peat.

GORDON TERRACE, EGGLESTON

53 The butcher's cart doing deliveries around Eggleston was recorded by O.H. Wicksteed. It consisted of a wooden cupboard with a rear opening and a space for the driver's seat, which seems primitive, even for the period between the wars. The cart is standing at Balmer House and would be doing the rounds for either Roy Walton at Romaldkirk or Harold Dowson at Mickleton. Dr. Wicksteed also remembered a dogcart in use at Eggleston. In the 1890s a Mrs. Robinson was a butcher and grocer at Eggleston.

54 The road to Woodland was pictured by one of the Hounams. Tom Todd, recalling his early years in Teesdale, remarks that 'carts were built substantial from chosen timber to withstand shaking, and were handed down from father to son. Mrs. Sherwood, who kept the Rose and Crown at Middleton-in-Teesdale towards the back end (autumn), used one of her brother's horses to lead sufficient coals from the Woodland pit to last over the winter. It was a biggish job as there were no coal depots in those days'. The road was turnpiked in 1808 from Hoodgate (Hude Gate) west of Middleton-in-Teesdale to the Edge near West Pitts, Woodland, with a branch to Eggleston Bridge. Milestones to Edge still survive to puzzle visitors. Tom used to get a bottle of nettle beer at Eggle-ston toll bar. John Bainbridge, born at Gate House, began a bottling business there with a gate moulded on the marble-stoppered bottles, and moved it into the village.

55 Posted in 1906, this view of Middleton-in-Teesdale from across the river overlooks Middleton station, the terminus of the Tees Valley Railway which opened in 1868. A single platform sufficed. Plans to continue to Alston were soon abandoned. The mineral line in the foreground carried men and whinstone setts, curbstones and road chippings from Middleton and Parkend quarries where hundreds of men were employed. Sidings also served limestone quarries. The first stationmaster planted the screening trees. The Cattle Mart had not yet come to County Bridge, and Middleton was still confined at the entrance to the much mined Hudeshope valley. At its height, around two hundred lead miners lived in the village and two hundred lodged at farms in the surrounding township.

56   The wide open space, now registered as a village green, was the Cattle Market. The Horse Market was along the front of the buildings opposite. Fairs for cattle, sheep and horses were discontinued at Middleton when one was established near High Force. In 1924 the Cattle Mart with permanent pens was set up beside the Tees at County Bridge. The arched building on the left is the Talbot Inn. Tom Todd took the inn for five years and recalled quoits, knur and spell and pitch and toss being played on the green, and a horse trough on the edge of the green. The Wesleyan Methodist Chapel of 1870 seated 400, replacing one of 1809. On the left, the cast iron drinking fountain, the 1875 memorial of the London Lead Company's agent R.W. Bainbridge, is just visible behind the tree. The green now has a walled edge and is landscaped. This view from the end of Hill Terrace is now obscured by parked cars and by the small new tree which is now fully mature.

Horse Market, Middleton-in-Teesdale.

57   On Fair Day at Middleton in 1911, horses show their paces, being walked or ridden along Horsemarket. They are starting at the road junction outside the Talbot Inn, at the hub of the village. Three Thursday fairs were held annually in March, April and September. The trees on the green are beginning to mature. There is a gaslamp by the shops and two can be detected at each end of the green. A gas manager was recorded in the 1861 Census Returns.

Fair Day Middleton 1911

58　From the road junction, with the Talbot Inn on the right, the entrance into Market Place reveals Middleton's older properties built before the lead mining boom of the 19th century. One lintel is dated IG1724. Some two-storey properties on the left are three or four at the rear down the steep bank of the Hudeshope Beck. Shops are in evidence. On the left centre, the taller double-fronted shop became Walter Willsons Ltd, and next door to the left was Longstaff's. Douglas Ramsden described how in the 1940s on Tuesdays and Saturdays a battered old bus, the Teesdale Queen, used to bring women from the scattered communities of the upper dale to shop in Middleton.

Market Place. Middleton-in-Teesdale

59 The road through Market Place divides at Seed Hill. It goes down left to Hude Bridge or up to the parish church of St. Mary, rebuilt in 1876, and onward to the lead mines of the Hudeshope valley. As befits a Market, and despite the Quaker and Non-Conformist influence, there were six inns in Middleton. The Blue Bell, now a house, was on the right next to the Cross Keys. The latter was renamed Ye Cleveland Arms when impressively rebuilt about 1890. The licensee was also a 'brake proprietor', no doubt offering visitors transport from the station and trips in the scenic dale. Later it became the Cleveland Arms Hotel with a livery stable of about twenty horses. It is now named the Teesdale Hotel. The Rose and Crown, built near Hude Bridge in 1742, is now a Working Men's Club. The Foresters' Arms and the King's Head remain in Market Place opposite Seed Hill. Barclays Bank (Backhouse's from 1856) replaced the premises on the right.

Market Place, Middleton-in-Teesdale.

60 Viewed from Seed Hill, the hanging signs of the Blue Bell and Ye Cleveland Arms show well. The old Town Hall opposite was built in 1847 by the Duke of Cleveland, who held manorial courts in it. The Mechanics Institute had its meetings and library there. The building had four round-headed windows above four open arches railed in for the butchers' stalls (shambles). It was extensively altered to open in 1911 as the Raby Estate Office for Teesdale. Cobbled areas remain. At Seed Hill, now registered as a village green, seeds and corn were sold. The stepped base and short pillar of the ancient Market Cross surmounted by a sundial is preserved here with the remains of the stocks. Below is a stone pump and water trough. Seed Hill was landscaped to celebrate Queen Elizabeth II's Silver Jubilee. The Trustee Savings Bank behind was built in 1842 as an early co-op, the Teesdale Workmen's Corn Association.

Market-Place, Middleton-in-Teesdale

61 Above and below Hude Bridge, on opposite banks, the Hudeshope Beck powered two corn mills. The mill house on the left with a fancy barge-board and garden has a young monkey puzzle (araucaria) tree, fashionable at the turn of the century and now grown to notable size. Pinkney's café was well-known to visitors and ramblers. A baker and confectioner, his many signboards let everyone know that Pinkney's Refreshment Rooms also sold ice cream, marmalade, hot pies, hot teas, Hovis bread and Rowntrees chocolate. A further attraction was the array of potted plants on top of the shop windows. This card was posted in 1904.

MIDDLETON-IN-TEESDALE. HUDE.

62   From Hude Bridge the steep ascent up the Hude gives an opportunity for panoramic views over Market Place from well above the rooftops of houses nearer the bridge. The horse and cart are following the ancient road up Teesdale. The present main road on lower ground was built in 1830 by the London Lead Company. These houses face a series of larger buildings across the road, comprising a Baptist chapel and Reading Room, 1827, seating 250, the old Police Station and the new Rectory 1829, now all turned to other uses. As the road levels out come the headquarters of the London Lead Company. A clock tower marks the entrance to their weighbridge, offices, smithy and carpenters' workshops. Beyond is Middleton House and Park. This card was posted in 1911.

Hude, Middleton-in-Teesdale.

63 The Middleton House card was posted in 1928. The London Lead Company bought the Middleton Estate in 1815, and developed mines from the 1820s. Middleton House was its northern headquarters and from 1880 its head office. It was built in 1823 to the design of Ignatius Bonomi of Durham, who also designed the model village of similar date at the other end of Middleton. The clock tower, workshops and stables came soon after. The house was the headquarters and residence of the Company's chief agent Robert Stagg, who created a park at the front and rear, changing 'an uneven boggy waste into smooth and beautiful lawns'. The Company's first school was built nearby, a National School with a library for miners attached. R.W. Bainbridge was the next agent. In the 1930s Middleton House was a shooting box of Lord Barnard, and after the war of Sir Joseph Nickerson. In the 1960s it was Middleton House Hotel.

COPYRIGHT
M.I.T. 61.

MIDDLETON HOUSE. MIDDLETON-IN-TEESDALE.

LILYWHITE LTD.
TRIANGLE HALIFAX

64   The London Lead Company built their second Middleton school in 1861. Its elaborate iron railings have gone. Trees and bushes now obscure it. After closure, Tom Todd, who had seen it built, converted it to an Assembly Hall seating 360. It had a stage, and was let for meetings, theatrical performances, church gatherings, concerts and dances. Travelling companies came for several days bringing their own scenery. Tea and supper parties were popular, with speeches followed by tea and an evening concert followed by coffee or a supper. The hall was also let to schools, and summer holiday groups came from Teesside and Wearside. After the First World War, Sunderland Education Authority bought it as a children's outdoor holiday centre. In the 1930s, however, it was still referred to as the Assembly Hall. It is now an Adventure Centre.

Sunderland School Camp, Middleton-in-Teesdale.

65 A whist drive, one of the many sociable activities held in Middleton Assembly Hall, was photographed in 1911 by D. Sinclair of Middleton. This card was posted in February 1918 to gunner J.B. Raine, Scotton Camp, Catterick, 'from your sister J.A. Raine'. The Ladies' Cloak Room is signposted on the right, whilst the stage is at the rear. A spade is displayed as the trumps for the game in progress. The printed bill on the left appears to announce a concert. A golf course at Middleton-in-Teesdale seems inconceivable, so doubtless the course at Barnard Castle would be used

Middleton Golf Club Whist Drive & Dance, Nov 29th 1911.

66 The Heather Brae Hotel at Snaisgill, near Middleton, stood near Monks Moor and had spectacular views into the Skears Beck valley, over Teesdale and into the Hudeshope valley. It was reached from Middleton Market Place by the road past the parish church and the Snaisgill Road, or via the King's Walk along woodland paths. A guide book of 1937 described it as 'a newly built moorland boarding house, a pleasant holiday home ... on the edge of the moors'. Now as Heatherbrae Retirement Home, it and its views are concealed behind a shelter belt of conifers.

HEATHER BRAE, MIDDLETON - IN - TEESDALE

67 Winch Bridge and Low Force waterfall on the Tees at Bowlees have long been a favourite place for visitors. The bridge across the little whinstone gorge, however, had a more mundane beginning, being made for travellers and more especially for miners. The first bridge on the site, erected in 1704, was believed the earliest suspension bridge on record. William Hutchinson described it as 'little more than two feet wide with a handrail on each side, and planked in such a manner that the traveller experiences all the tremulous motion of the chain and sees himself suspended over a roaring gulf, on an agitated, restless gangway, to which few strangers dare trust themselves'. In 1802, a chain snapped while local haymakers were crossing. Of three flung off, one died. The repaired bridge was replaced in 1830 by the stronger one seen here with calmer waters.

WINCH BRIDGE,
NEAR MIDDLETON-IN-TEESDALE

Nº1083.

68   By tradition, Willie Wilkinson gatecrashed the Duke of Cleveland's shooting party and begged for land for a chapel at Bowlees, which was at once granted. The first Primitive Methodist Chapel of 1824 was replaced in 1845 and enlarged in 1852 to seat 264. The present chapel was built on its site in 1868 when Teesdale lead mining and population were at their peak. It had a gallery and 530 seats. In 1904 the walls were lowered, the gallery removed, a schoolroom partitioned off and seating reduced to 250. In 1968 Newbiggin and Bowlees Methodist Trusts united. Bowlees Chapel closed in 1969 and the handsome organ, pulpit and communion rail went to Newbiggin, the country's oldest Methodist chapel still in continuous use. In 1975 Bowlees Chapel became an Interpretive Centre for Upper Teesdale managed by Durham Wildlife Trust. These changes encapsulate much of the recent history of the dale.

69   These men were probably working around Newbiggin or Bowlees. A typical Fordson tractor of the 1930s draws a reaper and binder to harvest a field of oats. Stalks severed by a scissor-like cutter are knocked down by the rotating bars on to a conveyor canvas, to be bound into sheaves by the knotter and discharged down a slide plate on to the ground. The men then pick up the sheaves and stand several together upright into stooks, as can be seen in the field behind. After drying out for a few days they are then taken to the rick or stack. The edges and corners of a field would be hand-cut with a scythe. During the last war, sheaves were spread around a field so as not to be lost through incendiaries. The boy and dog may be there to cartch rabbits as they escape from the last bit of standing corn. Oats have been grown in the dale up to 1,440 feet, though it was said they often didn't ripen.

70 This postcard photograph by D. Sinclair of Middleton-in-Teesdale is of uncle Harrison of Field Head Farm, Newbiggin. The farmstead stands near the beck in the small dale above the village and near the road which leads over the moors at Swinhope Head to Westgate in Weardale. Nearer the village and beside the same beck was a small old smelting mill, later used for making Victorian slate pencils. It was later converted into a row named Mill Houses.

71   Built as the Duke of Cleveland's shooting box, by 1847 it was a candle-lit inn with a visitors' book and a view of the Force from an upstairs sitting room. In the 1890s 'conveyances from Mr. John Coltman's High Force Hotel meet every train'. The livery stables had about twenty horses. In 1908 on Hotel ponies 'one can explore Mickle Fell, visit Cauldron Snout, and make acquaintance with Cronkley Scar and High Cup Nick ... but let it be remembered that they all lie out of the Beaten Tracks, and should be visited with as much Discrimination and Forethought as with Anticipation and Enthusiasm'. In the 1930s 'The inn is well known to bog-trotters and botanists' and 'a shuttle service of tub traps, wagonettes and brakes served the hotel, which provided refreshments for visitors and luke-warm gruel for the horses'. At one stage there were peacocks!. The Teesdale Fell Rescue Team is now based here.

HIGH FORCE HOTEL, MIDDLETON-IN-TEESDALE.

72   High Force in flood in September 1926, was one of those occasions more usual at the end of winter, when melting snows and heavy rain brought a wall of water careering down as the Tees Roll. Numerous disastrous floods have been recorded, one of the worst in 1771. Visitors caught unawares on the central rock have had to be rescued. Some have been swept to their death. Floods can still occur, despite a regulating reservoir at Cow Green. In his sketching tour of 1816, J.M.W. Turner met unrelenting downpours in Teesdale. His water-stained sketchbooks and paintings based on them show High Force in lively mood, one with a rainbow. Arther Young about 1770 recorded 'such a foam and misty rain that the sun never shines without a large and brilliant rainbow appearing ... the scene is truly sublime'.

High Force, September

73 West Underhurth Farm near Langdon Beck is a Raby Estate farm with traditional white limewash. In the 19th century the Estate rebuilt its old Teesdale longhouse farms (with house, barn, byre and stable in a row) and built new ones. Tenancies were virtually hereditary. The men and boys often worked in the lead mines whilst the women managed the farms and lodged miners. Smallholdings reached exceptional heights, with Manor Gill (Rumney's) and Grasshill Farms at almost 2,000 feet. Milk production has now given way to calf rearing. At High Hurth Edge, the limestone scar on the horizon, the Teesdale Cave, known as Hobthrush Hole, Fairy Hole or Moking Hurth Cave, was explored from 1878 by James Backhouse. He excavated the bones of a lynx, a wolf, other animals and birds and the skeleton of a woman believed of Iron Age date. A lime kiln burned the scar rock, above which Crow coal was got for local use.

74 An unknown party enjoy a moorland picnic. Had the man been fishing? William Hutchinson describes such an occasion at an earlier date beside the High Force. '... a party of pleasure, consisting of several gentlemen and ladies, sat enjoying the beauties of the scene: the rocks were spread with their repast, and the servant attending catched the living spring to mix their wine: deep in a grot they sat, shadowed with hanging oaks, which grew on the cliffs.'

75   Lead mining in the North Pennines met a rapid decline as lead prices dropped in the late 19th century. Abandoned workings littered the high fells. From Langdon Beck, Peghorn Lane led upward behind Widdybank Fell and continued north to Dubbysike and Greenhurth mines, rejoining the Middleton to Alston Road at its summit on Yad Moss. Greenhurth, or Greenearth, mine was still working when pictured here by James Backhouse in 1896. Some mid-19th-century working had been reopened by the Greenhurth Mining Company formed in 1868. The ore in the Greenhurth Vein was in the whin sill and remarkably rich. 18,000 tons of lead concentrates were produced before the mine was suddenly flooded out and closed in 1902.

76   Before Cow Green reservoir was built, this was the scene, the Weel, where the Tees meandered slowly over the tough whin sill until cascading down Cauldron Snout. The area was criss-crossed by mineral veins. Rod's Vein and Holmes Vein are opencast in the foreground. Cow Green mine was worked for barytes, barium sulphate, for a myriad industrial uses. Opened in 1935 by the Hedworth Barium Company, it was followed by the Wrentnall Barytes Company (renamed the Anglo-Austral Mining Company Ltd). Eight miners' cottages at Langdon Beck and the mine road were built in 1936-1938. Cow Green mine was over 600 feet deep and 15 feet wide. Electrified, it had a dressing plant, office, fitting shop and drying room. Closed in 1954, its remains were demolished in 1967 when reservoir building began. The distant dark boulder clay mounds were quarried to build the dam. This scene has vanished under a top water level at 1,603 feet.